Life is Great!

Life is Great!

A Gratitude Journal

MARY NG SHWU LING

authorHOUSE®

AuthorHouse™
1663 Liberty Drive
Bloomington, IN 47403
www.authorhouse.com
Phone: 1-800-839-8640

First published by AuthorHouse   07/19/2011

ISBN: 978-1-4634-3779-4 (sc)

Printed in the United States of America

Any people depicted in stock imagery provided by Thinkstock are models, and such images are being used for illustrative purposes only.
Certain stock imagery © Thinkstock.

This book is printed on acid-free paper.

Dedication

This book is specially dedicated to my nieces and nephews:

Clifton , Diane, Daphne, Priscilla, Joshua,
Johnathan, Bettina, Barnabas, Bethany and Bethea.

Thank you for the joy of fellowship each time we meet to
celebrate a special occasion!

Acknowledgement

I am eternally grateful to the team of publishers from AuthorHouse, Rey August, Laura Edwards, Cris Diaz, Tim Mendoza and team . . . for making the publication of this Gratitude Journal a joy!

A gratitude journal is a wonderful tool to capture beautiful thoughts of people, experiences, things and events in life which you are thankful for. It is also a very useful tool for pastors, mentors, counselors, teachers and parents to help their congregation, students, and children cultivate the attitude of a thankful heart.

Gratitude journaling is a process that can bring greater joy and better well being. It creates a personal process for expressing gratitude and indulge in the joyful act of giving thanks and appreciation for the blessings in life.

Gratitude has been said to have one of the strongest links to mental health of any character traits. It also develops self awareness to solving emotional and other problems. The process of gratitude journaling can help you heal old wounds and change your perspective in life. You will feel happier, enriched, inspired and this will show in the way you conduct yourself.

Numerous studies have found that people who are more grateful are less depressed, less stressed and more satisfied with their lives and relationships. They also have higher levels of control of their environments, personal growth, purpose in life and self acceptance. They are also less likely to be greedy or alcoholics and have greater resistance to viral infections.

Grateful people also have less negative coping strategies, being less likely to try to avoid the problem, deny there is a problem, blame themselves or cope through substance use. Grateful people also sleep better because they think more positive thoughts just before going to sleep.

Cultivating gratitude is also a form of cognitive behavioral therapy which holds that changing people's thought patterns can dramatically affect their moods.

Gratitude brings similar benefits in children and adolescents. Children who feel grateful tend to get better grades, set higher goals, complain of fewer headaches and stomach aches and feel more satisfied with their friends, family and schools than those who don't.

In the *Journal of Happiness Studies*, Froh and colleagues surveyed 1 035 high school students and found that the more grateful students had more friends and better health while the more materialistic students had lower grades, higher levels of envy and less satisfaction with life. Froh says, *"one of the best cure for materialism is to make somebody grateful for what he has."*

So start a daily habit of giving thanks by listing something that makes you smile or feel good. It can be as simple as having a glass of orange juice to quench your thirst, having a job to pay the bills or even having your memory so that you know your way home.

You will gain a new perspective on life as you reflect on the many blessings in your life. Your life will be transformed and empowered through the power of gratitude!

Mary Ng Shwu Ling

How to use this journal?

We all lead busy lives and take many things for granted. We spend our time doing many things but how often do we count our blessings?

Let's take time to reflect each day or week. What have you enjoyed today? What have made you happy and smile? Every day, there is something new to be thankful for. Is it a family member or friend, or simply a good night's sleep?

If you are still thinking hard, consider life's little joys like: the rain that refreshes the earth, a glass of berry juice or watching a movie on the weekend with your buddy. Use this journal to guide you in keeping track of the wonderful things you are grateful for.

This journal is designed to be used daily, weekly, or as and when you have something to be grateful for. Take a moment to reflect and write down three things you are grateful for at that moment. Then use the notes and quotes for further reflection. Build a journal of life's experiences. You can also add your favorite quotes, poems, songs and mementos.

You will find that once you start to reflect, you will see the many wonderful things to be grateful for and sense a wonderful joy of wellbeing and fulfillment.

Tips for gratitude:

There is good in every person and every situation.

All happy moments, both big and small, are worth being grateful for.

Make a goal to say something to lift up someone each day.

Whenever there is an opportunity, give a helping hand to someone in need.

(1st week)

Gratitude unlocks the fullness of life.
　　　　　　　—Melody Beattie

Life holds so many simple blessings, each day bringing its own individual wonder.
　　　　　　　—John McLeod

Every morning, when we wake up, it is a new day and one we should be grateful for to enjoy the blessings because life is great!
　　　　　　　—Mary Ng Shwu Ling

3 things that I am grateful for today:

1)

2)

3)

Reflections:

(2nd week)

Write a note, e-mail or a thank you card to someone you are grateful for. It could be your parents, a mentor, a teacher, a friend who laughed and cried with you, a colleague who stood by you, a volunteer who served with you, or even your spouse.

3 things that I am grateful for today:

1)

2)

3)

Reflections:

(3rd week)

Simply give others a bit of yourself, a thoughtful act, a helpful idea, a word of appreciation, a lift over a rough spot, a sense of understanding, a timely suggestion.—Charles H Burr

3 things that I am grateful for today:

1)

2)

3)

Reflections:

(4th week)

Feeling gratitude and not expressing it is like wrapping a present and not giving it.—William Arthur Ward

3 things that I am grateful for today:

1)

2)

3)

Reflections:

(5th week)

To speak gratitude is courteous and pleasant, to enact gratitude is generous and noble, but to live gratitude is to touch heaven.—Johannesburg A Gaetner

3 things that I am grateful for today:

1)

2)

3)

Reflections:

(6th week)

Expressing gratitude is a gift that enriches your life and uplifts your spirit.

3 things that I am grateful for today:

1)

2)

3)

Reflections:

(7th week)

Some people make lives brighter and our hearts lighter. Appreciate the ones around you who make a difference.—Anonymous

3 things that I am grateful for today:

1)

2)

3)

Reflections:

(8th week)

It is not what we have in our life, but who we have in our life that counts.—J M Lawrence

3 things that I am grateful for today:

1)

2)

3)

Reflections:

(9th week)

Affirmation:

I am grateful for all of the blessings I already have and am looking forward to accepting this continued blessings of goodness.

3 things that I am grateful for today:

1)

2)

3)

Reflections:

(10th week)

Life's ups and downs provide windows of opportunity to determine your values and goals. Think of using all obstacles as stepping stones to build the life you want.—Marsha Sinetar

Draw or sketch something you are grateful for.

3 things that I am grateful for today:

1)

2)

3)

Reflections:

(11th week)

Appreciation can make a day, even change a life.—Author Unknow

3 things that I am grateful for today:

1)

2)

3)

Reflections:

(12th week)

We have shelter, a home, a bed to sleep, food for every meal, friends and family who love us. These are all things we have taken for granted and yet without them, where will we be?

3 things that I am grateful for today:

1)

2)

3)

Reflections:

(13th week)

Turn your wounds into wisdom.—Oprah Winfrey

Gratitude journaling helps to remind us that we have much to be grateful for . . . Even our problems can be a source of thankfulness when we view it from a different perspective.

3 things that I am grateful for today:

1)

2)

3)

Reflections:

(14th week)

We should be grateful for experiencing difficult times for they help us to grow spiritually and mentally.

3 things that I am grateful for today:

1)

2)

3)

Reflections:

(15th week)

Difficult times also teach us by providing new experiences which we can help and share with others when they are facing the crises.

3 things that I am grateful for today:

1)

2)

3)

Reflections:

(16th week)

Difficult times also allow us to appreciate what we already have all the more.

3 things that I am grateful for today:

1)

2)

3)

Reflections:

(17th week)

Gratitude thoughts reveals to us that by finding a way to be grateful for our troubles, we can turn the negatives into positive blessings.

3 things that I am grateful for today:

1)

2)

3)

Reflections:

(18th week)

This week, say thank you to the people you love. Be grateful for the sunshine, friends and family. Enjoy the warmth of the sun on your skin and go out with your friends for a picnic or just cycle around the neighborhood with your family.

3 things that I am grateful for today:

1)

2)

3)

Reflections:

(19th week)

Being grateful for even the smallest things can open doors to a richer world.

Be grateful for doctors, nurses and hospital. They are very important for those who are sick.

3 things that I am grateful for today:

1)

2)

3)

Reflections:

(20th week)

Write a poem on some event or situation which you are grateful for.

Be grateful for celebrities, business people and all others who contributed generously to charities.

3 things that I am grateful for today:

1)

2)

3)

Reflections:

(21st week)

The more you find to be thankful for, the more things come your way that you can be grateful about and happy for . . . It is like a snowball effect.

3 things that I am grateful for today:

1)

2)

3)

Reflections:

(22nd week)

Be grateful for your job because you can pay the bills through the money earned.

3 things that I am grateful for today:

1)

2)

3)

Reflections:

(23rd week)

Be thankful that you don't already have everything you desire. If you did, what would there be to look forward to?

3 things that I am grateful for today:

1)

2)

3)

Reflections:

(24th week)

Be thankful when you don't know something. For it gives you the opportunity to learn something new.

3 things that I am grateful for today:

1)

2)

3)

Reflections:

(25th week)

Be thankful for the rain that refreshes the earth.

3 things that I am grateful for today:

1)

2)

3)

Reflections:

(26th week)

Be thankful for your limitations because they give you opportunities for improvement.

3 things that I am grateful for today:

1)

2)

3)

Reflections:

(27th week)

Buy a thank you gift for someone you are grateful for.

3 things that I am grateful for today:

1)

2)

3)

Reflections:

(28th week)

My cancer scare changed my life. I'm grateful for every new, healthy day I have. It has helped me prioritize my life.—Olivia Newton-John

Be thankful for each challenge because it will build your strength and character. I know of people who are happier despite lower incomes, smaller homes and simpler lifestyles because of their new focus on what really matters in life.

They shared about the new lives they have come to accept and enjoy after chronic illness, accidents, losing loved ones, losing their jobs or other challenges. Some were victims of a crime, tsunami, crisis and some are living with incurable illnesses or disabilities.

They shared about finding inner strength, support from friends and relatives, marriages being strengthened in the face of adversity and even rediscovering the joys of family bonding through difficult times in their life.

Some are even reassessing their lives and needs, thinking about what really matters in life and realizing how blessed they really are.

We have no right to ask when sorrow comes, "why did this happen to me?" unless we ask the same question for every moment of happiness that comes our way.—Author Unknown

There's no disaster that can't become a blessing . . .—Richard Bach

A crisis is an opportunity riding the dangerous wind.—Chinese Proverb

3 things that I am grateful for today:

1)

2)

3)

Reflections:

(29th week)

Be thankful for your mistakes because they will teach you valuable lessons.

3 things that I am grateful for today:

1)

2)

3)

Reflections:

(30th week)

Be thankful when you are tired because it means that you have worked hard and contributed to society.

3 things that I am grateful for today:

1)

2)

3)

Reflections:

(31st week)

For today and it's blessings, I owe the world an attitude of gratitude.—Anonymous

Be thankful for your job because it makes you skillful and useful.

3 things that I am grateful for today:

1)

2)

3)

Reflections:

(32nd week)

If you count all your assets, you always show a profit.—Robert Quillen

Be thankful that you have made a positive difference in other people's life through your work.

3 things that I am grateful for today:

1)

2)

3)

Reflections:

(33rd week)

What seem to us bitter trials are often blessings in disguise.—Oscar Wilde

It is easy to be thankful for the good things in life—a life of rich fulfillment comes to those who are also thankful for the setbacks.

Birds sing after a storm; why shouldn't people feel as free to delight in whatever remains to them?—Rose F. Kennedy

3 things that I am grateful for today:

1)

2)

3)

Reflections:

(34th week)

The difficulties, hardships and trials of life . . . Are positive blessings. They knit the muscles more firmly, and teach self-reliance.—William Matthews

Gratitude can turn a negative into a positive. Find a way to be thankful for your troubles and they can become your blessings.

3 things that I am grateful for today:

1)

2)

3)

Reflections:

(35th week)

Gratitude is a thing to be practiced, like the piano.—Mary Ng Shwu Ling

Has your outlook on life changed for the better since you have begin looking at all the things you can be thankful for?

3 things that I am grateful for today:

1)

2)

3)

Reflections:

(36th week)

Be grateful for memory cause without it you may not know your way home.

3 things that I am grateful for today:

1)

2)

3)

Reflections:

(37th week)

Be grateful for your home or you would be sleeping on the streets.

3 things that I am grateful for today:

1)

2)

3)

Reflections:

(38th week)

I am beginning to learn that it is the sweet, simple things of life which are the real ones after all.—Laura Ingalls Wilder

Invite a person whom you are grateful for out for a meal to show your appreciation. The person could be your role model, mentor or even counselor.

Be grateful for your boss or else you will not be hired and there will be no pay day.

3 things that I am grateful for today:

1)

2)

3)

Reflections:

(39th week)

Without the illness I would never have been forced to re-evaluate my life and my career.—Lance Armstrong

Be grateful for your health, otherwise you will be suffering in bed and have to worry about your medical bills.

3 things that I am grateful for today:

1)

2)

3)

Reflections:

(40th week)

Be grateful for your parents or else you would not be here today.

Life is what we make it, always has been, always will be.—Grandma Moses

3 things that I am grateful for today:

1)

2)

3)

Reflections:

(41st week)

Be grateful for your computer, iPad, laptop, iPhone and the Internet where you can have access to information speedily.

3 things that I am grateful for today:

1)

2)

3)

Reflections:

(42nd week)

Be grateful for electricity or else all the electrical appliances would not work.

3 things that I am grateful for today:

1)

2)

3)

Reflections:

(43rd week)

Be grateful for clean water to bathe, wash, cook and drink.

3 things that I am grateful for today:

1)

2)

3)

Reflections:

(44th week)

Be grateful for the shopping malls in your neighborhood which you do not have to travel far to enjoy retail therapy.

3 things that I am grateful for today:

1)

2)

3)

Reflections:

(45th week)

We all have big changes in our lives that are more or less a second chance.—Harrison Ford

Be grateful for those who were patient with us and gave us a second chance.

3 things that I am grateful for today:

1)

2)

3)

Reflections:

(46th week)

Be grateful for music which inspires and relaxes you.

Be grateful for musicians and composers.

(47th week)

Be grateful for the rubbish collector or else the whole neighborhood will be like a rubbish dump.

3 things that I am grateful for today:

1)

2)

3)

Reflections:

(48th week)

Gratitude is not only the greatest of virtues, but the parent of all the others.—Cicero

3 things that I am grateful for today:

1)

2)

3)

Reflections:

(49th week)

Be grateful for hunger and thirst. Be attuned to these sensations this week and appreciate how your body lets you know what you need and when you need it.

3 things that I am grateful for today:

1)

2)

3)

Reflections:

(50th week)

One of the secrets of life is to make stepping stones out of stumbling blocks.—Jack Penn

Be grateful for pain. It protects us from hurting ourselves further when we sense it and tells us when it is time to seek help. Imagine what would happen if we could put our hands above a stove without feeling pain.

3 things that I am grateful for today:

1)

2)

3)

Reflections:

(51st week)

Take a photograph of the person or thing you are grateful for and post it on your Facebook.

3 things that I am grateful for today:

1)

2)

3)

Reflections:

(52nd week)

Make a collage of all the things that you are grateful for this week with a happy picture of yourself in the middle.

3 things that I am grateful for today:

1)

2)

3)

Reflections:

Suggested reading:

Encyclopedia of Gratitude by Erich Origen

If you wish to contact the author,

email her at **maryng64@hotmail.com**.